Never Alone

WRITTEN AND COMPILED BY

RUTH HARLEY

DESIGNED AND ILLUSTRATED BY KATHY TRAVERS

PUBLISHED BY THE C.R. GIBSON COMPANY
NORWALK, CONNECTICUT

CONTENTS

FORWARD

From David, the Biblical shepherd boy singing in the field, to the Apollo astronaut journeying through the void of space, there is a continuous thread of feeling that ties us together. Each of us has felt loneliness.

"Why must it happen to me?" you may ask.

"Why have I been chosen to suffer this feeling? Why me?"

Or perhaps, "How can I face this loneliness? How can I stand to live apart while the world goes on, forgetting that I exist? Doesn't anyone care about me?"

Before you decide that you have been so singled out, listen. There is one voice saying, "Lo, I am with you always . . ." It is the voice of Jesus.

And there are other voices speaking to you. Throughout the ages, people have faced the grief of loneliness. Many have experienced the loneliness of spiritual isolation. Others have been physically abandoned by those they trusted. A few of these people have had the ability to express their feelings eloquently in poetry or prose. Some of their thoughts are in the pages of this book.

Let those who have been lonely reach out through time and space to give you the strength that comes from courage and the comfort that comes from understanding.

You are never alone.

TO BE ALONE

Even as a small boy, C. Austin Miles loved music. He was only twelve when he was called upon to substitute for the church organist in a rural New Jersey church. Austin went on to get a degree in pharmacy but, after working as a pharmacist for ten years, he returned to the University of Pennsylvania to study music. In 1898, he gave up pharmacy altogether and devoted his full time to music. He was the author or composer of nearly 3,000 hymns.

In his "In the Garden," Miles pictures Mary Magdalene coming to the Garden of the Resurrection early on the first day of the week and approaching the sepulchre.

Miles wrote the hymn in 1912 and sold it for the sum total of four dollars. During Miles's lifetime, more than 3 million copies of the hymn were sold in sheet music and more than 1 million recordings were made. It is still sung in many languages.

In The Garden

I come to the garden alone,
While the dew is still on the roses:
And the voice I hear,
Falling on my ear,
The Son of God discloses.

He speaks, and the sound of His voice
Is so sweet, the birds hush their singing,
And the melody,
That He gave to me,
Within my heart is ringing.

I'd stay in the garden with Him,
Tho' the night around me be falling,
But He bids me go:
Throu' the voice of woe,
His voice to me is calling.

Refrain:
And He walks with me, and He talks with me,
And He tells me I am His own:
And the joy we share, as we tarry there,
None other has ever known.

C. Austin Miles

Joseph Medlicott Scriven, an Englishman who wrote the hymn "What a Friend We Have in Jesus," experienced many disappointments in his life. He was forced to discontinue his education as an army officer because of ill health. Then, on the evening before he was to be married, his fiancée accidentally drowned.

Still only twenty-five years old, Scriven moved to Canada where he became a tutor and schoolteacher. He was once again engaged to be married, this time to Eliza Roche, but Miss Roche suddenly died before they could be married.

In spite of his grief, Scriven was still able to declare, "What a Friend We Have in Jesus." He wrote the words to this hymn for his mother during a time of sorrow. When he died, the hymn was found near his bedside.

What A Friend We Have In Jesus

What a friend we have in Jesus,
All our sins and griefs to bear!
What a privilege to carry
Everything to God in prayer!
O what peace we often forfeit,
O what needless pain we bear,
All because we do not carry
Everything to God in prayer!

Have we trials and temptations?
Is there trouble anywhere?
We should never be discouraged:
Take it to the Lord in prayer!
Can we find a friend so faithful
Who will all our sorrows share?
Jesus knows our every weakness —
Take it to the Lord in prayer!

Are we weak and heavy-laden,
Cumbered with a load of care?
Precious Savior, still our refuge —
Take it to the Lord in prayer!
Do thy friends despise, forsake thee?
Take it to the Lord in prayer!
In his arms he'll take and shield thee,
Thou wilt find a solace there.

Joseph M. Scriven (1820 - 1886)

10

David, the shepherd boy who later became King of Judah and Israel, was the youngest in a family of eight sons, and he often had the task of watching the sheep. When he was out in the fields with his flock, he would play his simple harp. In later years, having become a skilled musician, David composed songs of praise, or *psalms*, which assert his unswerving faith in the providence of God.

PSALM 23

The Lord is my shepherd;
I shall not want.

He maketh me to lie down in green pastures: he leadeth me beside the still waters.

He restoreth my soul: he leadeth me in the paths of righteousness for his name's sake.

Yea, though I walk through the valley of the shadow of death, I will fear no evil: for thou art with me; thy rod and thy staff they comfort me.

Thou preparest a table before me in the presence of mine enemies: thou anointest my head with oil; my cup runneth over.

Surely goodness and mercy shall follow me all the days of my life: and I will dwell in the house of the Lord for ever.

A Psalm of David

PSALM 138

I will praise thee with my whole heart: before the gods will I sing praise unto thee.

I will worship toward thy holy temple, and praise thy name for thy lovingkindness and for thy truth: for thou hast magnified thy word above all thy name.

In the day when I cried thou answeredst me, and strengthenedst me with strength in my soul.

All the kings of the earth shall praise thee, O Lord, when they hear the words of thy mouth.

Yea, they shall sing in the ways of the Lord: for great is the glory of the Lord.

Though the Lord be high, yet hath he respect unto the lowly: but the proud he knoweth afar off.

Though I walk in the midst of trouble, thou wilt revive me: thou shalt stretch forth thine hand against the wrath of mine enemies, and thy right hand shall save me.

The Lord will perfect that which concerneth me: thy mercy, O Lord, endureth for ever: forsake not the works of thine own hands.

A Psalm of David

In 1932, Anne Morrow Lindbergh was pregnant with her second child when her first son, Charles A. Lindbergh, Jr., aged twenty-one months, was kidnapped. After weeks of agonizing suspense, the kidnapped child's body was found near the Lindberghs' New Jersey home. Even then the ordeal was not over for the Lindberghs. The tracking down of the kidnapper, the trial, and the relentless glare of publicity continued through 1935.

Forty years later, Mrs. Lindbergh published the diaries she had kept at the time in her book *Hour of Gold, Hour of Lead.* In the paragraphs that follow, she expresses some of her thoughts as she looks back at her tragic experience.

Suffering is certainly individual, but at the same time it is a universal experience. There are even certain familiar stages in suffering, and familiar, if not identical, steps in coming to terms with it, as in the healing of illness — as, in fact, coming to terms with death itself. To see these steps in another's life can be illuminating and perhaps even helpful.

What I am saying is not simply the old Puritan truism that "suffering teaches." I do not believe that sheer suffering teaches. If suffering alone taught, all the world would be wise, since everyone suffers. To suffering must be added mourning, understanding, patience, love, openness, and the willingness to remain vulnerable. All these and other factors combined, if the circumstances are right, *can* teach and can lead to rebirth.

But there is no simple formula, or swift way out, no comfort, or easy acceptance of suffering . . .

. . . Undoubtedly, the long road of suffering, insight, healing, or rebirth, is best illustrated in the Christian religion by the suffering, death, and resurrection of Christ. It is also illustrated by the story of Buddha's answer to a mother who had lost her child. According to the legend, he said that to be healed she needed only a mustard seed from a household that had never known sorrow. The woman journeyed from home to home over the world but never found a family ignorant of grief. Instead, in the paradoxical manner of myths and oracles, she found truth, understanding, compassion, and eventually, one feels sure, rebirth.

Anne Morrow Lindbergh (1907 -   )

Over a century ago, a concerned young Welsh woman was visiting the English prisons at Bristol and working to aid the prisoners after they were discharged. Anna Laetitia Waring was not only a social worker, she was also a poet. She had been brought up in the Society of Friends, but later joined the Church of England.

In 1850, Miss Waring published a collection, *Hymns and Meditations by A.L.W.*, which contained nineteen hymns. It was later expanded to include thirty-nine hymns which she had written. Many of them show her strong belief that God can be a companion, regardless of one's surroundings or circumstances.

In Heavenly Love Abiding

In heavenly love abiding,
No change my heart shall fear:
And safe is such confiding,
For nothing changes here.
The storm may roar without me,
My heart may low be laid;
But God is round about me,
And can I be dismayed?

Wherever he may guide me,
No want shall turn me back:
My Shepherd is beside me,
And nothing can I lack.
His wisdom ever waketh,
His sight is never dim:
He knows the way he taketh,
And I will walk with him.

Green pastures are before me,
Which yet I have not seen:
Bright skies will soon be o'er me,
Where darkest clouds have been.
My hope I cannot measure,
My path to life is free:
My Savior has my treasure,
And he will walk with me.

Anna L. Waring (1823 - 1910)

. . . from PSALM 147

Praise ye the Lord: for it is good to sing praises unto our God: for it is pleasant; and praise is comely . . .

He healeth the broken in heart, and bindeth up their wounds.

He telleth the number of the stars: he calleth them all by their names.

Great is our Lord, and of great power: his understanding is infinite.

The Lord lifteth up the meek: he casteth the wicked down to the ground.

Sing unto the Lord with thanksgiving; sing praise upon the harp unto our God:

Who covereth the heaven with clouds, who prepareth rain for the earth, who maketh grass to grow upon the mountains . . .

The Lord taketh pleasure in them that fear him, in those that hope in his mercy . . .

Praise ye the Lord.

No One Loves You So

Do you think in your sorrow you suffer alone?
All your grief and your sadness to Him are made known:
He hath never forsaken, or turned from His own;
There is no one who loves you so.

Refrain:
There is no one who loves you like Jesus,
No one who loves you so;
For the cross you lay down
He will give you a crown;
There is no one who loves you so.

Alfred Barratt

William Cowper, the gifted English poet, studied law and was admitted to the bar, but he never practiced. He spent the most productive period of his life at Olney where he lived with the Reverend John Newton and his family. The poet and the pastor collaborated in writing hymns and published the famous *Olney Hymns*, sixty-seven of which were the work of Cowper.

Plagued by mental illness, Cowper periodically suffered deep periods of depression when he was unable to work. He felt that God had spared his life and many of his hymns reflect this belief. "God Moves in a Mysterious Way" is one of them.

God Moves In A Mysterious Way

God moves in a mysterious way
His wonders to perform;
He plants his footsteps in the sea,
And rides upon the storm.

Deep in unfathomable mines
Of never-failing skill
He treasures up his bright designs,
And works his sovereign will.

Ye fearful saints, fresh courage take;
The clouds ye so much dread
Are big with mercy, and shall break
In blessings on your head.

Judge not the Lord by feeble sense,
But trust him for his grace;
Behind a frowning providence
He hides a smiling face.

Blind unbelief is sure to err,
And scan his work in vain:
God is his own interpreter,
And he will make it plain.

William Cowper (1731 - 1800)

19

LET YOUR HEART
LOOK UP

During the long antarctic winter night of 1934, the Bolling Advance Weather Base on the Ross Ice Barrier was manned by a solitary person — Richard E. Byrd. The base was at the bottom of the world, 400 miles south of Little America. It could be reached only by tractor during the antarctic summer, and could not be reached at all during the stormy winter. (The helicopter had not yet been invented.)

It had been Byrd's own decision to remain by himself at the advance base. He reasoned that two men, living in the cramped confines of a shack for seven months, would certainly come to hate each other. Three would be the classic number but the limited space in the shack and the problem of carrying supplies for three men across the treacherous ice led Byrd to make his final choice. One man would have to stay alone and he refused to ask anyone to volunteer for a risk he was not prepared to take himself. He would be the man.

In the paragraphs that follow from Byrd's book *Alone,* he describes his initial adjustment to the situation.

A man can isolate himself from habits and conveniences — deliberately, as I have done; or accidentally, as a shipwrecked sailor might — and force his mind to forget. But the body is not so easily sidetracked. It keeps on remembering. Habit has set up in the core of the being a system of automatic physico-chemical actions and reactions which insist upon replenishment. That is where the conflict arises. I don't think that a man can do without sounds and smells and voices and touch, any more than he can do without phosphorus and calcium.

So I learned at Latitude 80°08′ South. It was exhilarating to stand on the Barrier and contemplate the sky and luxuriate in a beauty I did not aspire to possess. In the presence of such beauty we are lifted above natural crassness. And it was a fine thing, too, to surrender to the illusion of intellectual disembodiment, to feel the mind go voyaging through space as smoothly and felicitiously as it passes through the objects of its reflections. The body stood still, but the mind was free. It could travel the universe with the audacious mobility of a Wellesian time-space machine.

The senses were isolated in soundless dark; so, for that matter, was the mind; but one was stayed, while the other possessed the flight of a falcon: and the free choice and opportunity of the one everlastingly emphasized the poverty of the other. From the depth of my being would sometimes surge a fierce desire to be projected spectacularly into the living warmths and movements the mind revisited. Usually the desire had no special focus. It sought no single thing. Rather it darted and wavered over a panorama of human aspects — my family at dinner time, the sound of voices in a downstairs room, the cool feeling of rain.

. . . what I did, or tried to do, was to focus my thinking on healthy, constructive images and concepts and thus crowd out the unhealthy ones. I built a wall between myself and the past in an effort to extract every ounce of diversion and creativeness inherent in my immediate surroundings. Every day I experimented with new schemes for increasing the content of the hours. "A grateful environment," according to Santayana, "is a substitute for happiness." for it can stimulate us from without just as good works can stimulate us from within. My environment was instrinsically treacherous and difficult, but I saw ways to make it agreeable. I tried to cook more rapidly, take weather and auroral observations more expertly, and do routine things systematically. Full mastery of the impinging moment was my goal. I lengthened my walks and did more reading, and kept my thoughts upon an impersonal plane. In other words, I tried resolutely to attend to my business.

Richard E. Byrd (1885 - 1957)

In 1934, attractive young Betsey Barton was seriously injured in an automobile accident and her legs were permanently paralyzed. Years later she wrote a book entitled *And Now To Live Again* with the idea that it might help others. She wrote:

"There are, it seems to me, two tragic facts in human existence: We do not appreciate what we have until we lose it. And we only advance through suffering.

"A man must indeed lose his life to find it — to appreciate what he has lost more fully. And we are awakened and sensitized to the beauty and preciousness of life, to the mysterious and implacable rules by which it was planned for us by a guiding spirit, only through suffering.

". . . the person who was denied, the person who lost and fell behind in the race with the others, will, like the tortoise, come out ahead. For he will have grown in vision. He will know the value of what he has lost and of what he has dared to regain. And, through his new and wiser eyes, he will see that although he lost one life, he has won a new life that in many delicate and tender ways is a far better one.

"Had I read this years ago when first I lost the use of my legs, I would have thrown down the book in disgust. I was not ready then for any such philosophical phrases. There seemed to be no existing compensation for a boy who has lost a leg, for a child who is born a spastic, for the man who has tuberculosis, or for a girl who cannot move her hand. Yet it has been pressed in upon me that the power which created us, provided for this, too: for faith in the face of despair, for courage in the face of loss, and for tenderness in the face of hopelessness. We are never, we cannot be left alone. We are taken care of, if we allow ourselves to be, and the law of compensation is a fact. He who loses his life can find it, in the fullest and most complete sense of the word 'find.' "

"It takes time, but it will come, it must come — the ability to see and bear with what has happened, and now to move ahead. It will come always if we can start slowly enough with the few little things we are able to do, and begin to build on them. Not looking back: not looking ahead, but working steadily *now*. If we are faithful over these first few things, we will be rewarded. If we are faithful, we will become able, finally, to do much more. And if there are ninety-nine things missing and lost and only one present and found, let us try to remember the one that is present and build upon it."

James Montgomery was the son of Moravian missionaries who left him behind in England while they were serving in the West Indies. When his schoolmaster discovered that young James was wasting his time writing poetry, the boy was sent to serve as an apprentice to a baker.

Fortunately, James' interest in poetry was not discouraged. He became a champion of many worthwhile causes and expressed his sentiments in poems and hymns. In all, he wrote about 400 hymns with approximately 25 still in use today. One of them is "God Is My Strong Salvation."

God Is My Strong Salvation

God is my strong salvation:
What foe have I to fear?
In darkness and temptation,
My light, my help is near.

Though hosts encamp around me,
Firm in the fight I stand;
What terror can confound me,
With God at my right hand?

Place on the Lord reliance;
My soul, with courage wait;
His truth be thine affiance,
When faint and desolate.

His might thy heart shall strengthen,
His love thy joy increase;
Mercy thy days shall lengthen;
The Lord will give thee peace.

James Montgomery (1771 - 1854)

It was not until after his death that the world came to know the real Dag Hammarskjold. Secretary-General of the United Nations from 1953 to 1961, Hammarskjold was a member of one of Sweden's oldest aristocratic families with a long history of government service.

As Secretary-General, Hammarskjold felt the role included serving as a trusted consultant to all sides in any conflict. It was this belief that took him to Africa in 1961 to mediate between the various factions of the dispute in the Congo.

Flying from Leopoldville to Ndola in Northern Rhodesia, Hammarskjold's plane crashed in the jungle, eight miles from the airport, and he was killed.

After his death, a journal was found in which this remarkable man had recorded not the daily events of his life, but his thoughts and philosophy. Called *Markings*, it was published in 1964.

Hallowed be Thy name,
    not mine,
Thy kingdom come,
    not mine,
Thy will be done,
    not mine,
Give us peace with Thee
  Peace with men
  Peace with ourselves,
And free us from all fear.

Do not look back. And do not dream about the future, either. It will neither give you back the past, nor satisfy your other daydreams. Your duty, your reward — your destiny — are *here* and *now.*

What makes loneliness and anguish
Is not that I have no one to share my burden,
But this:
I have only my own burden to bear.

Pray that your loneliness may spur you into finding something to live for, great enough to die for.

Did'st Thou give me this inescapable loneliness so that it would be easier for me to give Thee all?

Dag Hammarskjold (1905 - 1961)

"God will care for and preserve His own in His own time," Georg Neumark decided about the year 1641. The young German student had just gone through a difficult time that restored his faith in the Lord. He had been en route to the Michaelmas Fair at Leipzig with a group of merchants when they were waylaid by a band of highwaymen. Neumark was robbed of everything but his prayerbook and a little money that was sewn in his clothing.

Neumark began to search for work in order to earn money to finish his education. He went from town to town, growing more and more discouraged. At last, in the city of Kiel, he was engaged as a tutor in the family of a wealthy judge. It was then that he wrote the hymn, "If Thou But Suffer God to Guide Thee."

After two years of tutoring, Neumark had saved enough money to go on with his schooling at Königsberg where he studied law.

If Thou But Suffer God To Guide Thee

If thou but suffer God to guide thee,
And hope in him through all thy ways,
He'll give thee strength, what-e'er betide thee,
And bear thee through the evil days;
Who trusts in God's unchanging love
Builds on the rock that naught can move.

Only be still, and wait his leisure
In cheerful hope, with heart content
To take what-e'er thy Father's pleasure
And all-deserving love hath sent;
Nor doubt our inmost wants are known
To him who chose us for his own.

Sing, pray, and keep his ways unswerving;
So do thine own part faithfully,
And trust his word, though undeserving;
Thou yet shalt find it true for thee;
God never yet forsook at need
The soul that trusted him indeed.

Georg Neumark (1621 - 1681)

Deafness, like other handicaps, can impose isolation. For a person who loses his hearing, isolation can be overpowering. Outnumbered in society 999 to 1, a deafened person must learn to live with himself and his limitations. In reality, all of us must.

Kenneth R. Lane became totally deaf at the age of sixteen from spinal meningitis. He now lives a busy life as an editor and travels widely to hold workshops for teachers and parents at conventions and schools for the deaf. He is also a freelance outdoor writer and professional fisherman. "Real isolation," he says, "is but a mental monster that drugs the mind."

On Facing Isolation

The silent wilderness of tamarack trees and cloud-dotted azure sky provided my only company. Ahead of me, up a gray shale rock mountain trail, lay a quiet lake in the White Pass area of the state of Washington. Thirty days hence I would be picked up at this same road-end spot.

The imposed isolation was the wisdom of my father. He reasoned that a sixteen-year-old, suddenly deafened by illness, needs to come to terms with himself. For thirty days I cooked,

slept fitfully, chopped wood, fished, sang, and cried. And I thought.

During those thirty days, a larva emerged to a pupa. The experience smoothed the metamorphosis from pupa to adulthood. Learning to live with oneself is the key essential for happiness.

Almost thirty years later, I now find myself selfishly planning time in which to be alone — isolated! My physical handicap may sometimes prove an inconvenience: society may isolate my body — but my mind is free. And as John Milton once penned, "The mind is its own place, and in itself Can make heaven of hell, a hell of heaven."

Kenneth R. Lane

A poem by *Samuel* Longfellow? Today, seeing a hymn written by S. Longfellow we are inclined to think that the "S." is an error. Actually, Samuel was the famous Henry Wadsworth Longfellow's younger brother. He was a graduate of Harvard University and Harvard Divinity School and an ordained minister of the Unitarian Church. His writings might have been totally eclipsed by those of his brother were it not for his numerous hymns. Many of them are still widely sung and loved, a century after they were written. One of these is "I Look To Thee in Every Need."

I Look To Thee In Every Need

I look to thee in every need,
And never look in vain;
I feel thy strong and tender love,
And all is well again:
The thought of thee is mightier far
Than sin and pain and sorrow are.

Discouraged in the work of life,
Disheartened by its load,
Shamed by its failures or its fears,
I sink beside the road;
But let me only think of thee,
And then new heart springs up in me.

Thy calmness bends serene above,
My restlessness to still;
Around me flows thy quickening life,
To nerve my faltering will:
Thy presence fills my solitude;
Thy providence turns all to good.

Embosomed deep in thy dear love,
Held in thy law, I stand;
Thy hand in all things I behold,
And all things in thy hand;
Thou leadest me by unsought ways
And turn'st my mourning into praise.

Samuel Longfellow (1819 - 1892)

On the three-man Apollo II flight to the moon in 1969, one astronaut, Michael Collins, had the assignment of remaining aboard the *Columbia* spacecraft to orbit the moon, while the other two astronauts — Edwin Aldrin, Jr., and Neil Armstrong — descended to the surface of the moon in the lunar module. Later Collins wrote in his book, *Carrying the Fire:*

"I don't mean to deny a feeling of solitude. It is there, reinforced by the fact that radio contact with the earth abruptly cuts off at the instant I disappear behind the moon. I am alone now, truly alone, and absolutely isolated from any known life. I am it. If a count were taken the score would be three billion plus two over on the other side of the moon, and one plus God only knows what on this side. I feel this powerfully — not as fear or loneliness — but as awareness, anticipation, satisfaction, confidence, almost exultation. I like the feeling. Outside my window I can see stars — and that is all. Where I know the moon to be, there is simply a black void: the moon's presence is defined solely by the absence of stars."

Later, after Aldrin and Armstrong have landed on the moon and taken their first walk on its surface, Collins continues to orbit, alone in the *Columbia.* His narrative goes on:

"It's time for me to douse the lights and get some sleep. Sleep? Alone by myself? You'd better believe it. These are familiar surroundings . . . As I scurry about, blocking off the windows with metal plates and dousing the lights, I have almost the same feeling that I used to have years ago when, as an altar boy, I snuffed the candles one by one at the end of a long service. Come to think of it, with the center couch removed, *Columbia's* floor plan is not unlike that of the National Cathedral, where I used to serve. Certainly it is cruciform with the tunnel up above where the bell tower would be, and the navigation instruments at the altar. The main instrument panels span the north and south transepts, while the nave is where the center couch used to be. If not a miniature cathedral, then at least it is a happy home, and I have no hesitation about leaving its care to God and Houston as I fade away into a comfortable snooze."

The fate of Amelia Earhart, the famous aviator, remains an enigma to this day. Her plane disappeared mysteriously in the Pacific in 1937. Since that time, numerous theories have been advanced to explain the incident. None has been proved.

Amelia Earhart knew what it was to be alone. In a physical sense, she was accustomed to flying solo, away from the crowd. She was alone in another sense too. She was one of the first women to dare to be independent in the male-dominated world of flying. Her brief poem "Courage" tells us a little more about her.

Courage

Courage is the price life exacts for granting peace.
The soul that knows it not, knows no release
    From little things;

Knows not the livid loneliness of fear
Nor mountain heights, where bitter joy can hear
    The sound of wings.

How can life grant us boon of living, compensate
For dull gray ugliness and pregnant hate
    Unless we dare

The soul's dominion? Each time we make a choice, we pay
With courage to behold resistless day
    And count it fair.

Amelia Earhart (1898 - 1937?)

. . . from PSALM 27

The Lord is my light and my salvation; whom shall I fear? the Lord is the strength of my life; of whom shall I be afraid?

. . . Wait on the Lord: be of good courage, and he shall strengthen thine heart: wait, I say, on the Lord.

A Psalm of David

Alone.

The word itself has a cold, isolated look about it. Solitude can be frightening, if we are also lonely. But to Henry David Thoreau, the 19th Century American author and naturalist, there was nothing frightening about solitude. Indeed, he sought it out.

For two years, Thoreau lived in a hut by himself on the shores of Walden Pond in Massachusetts. Some of his observations about living alone may be encouraging to one who suddenly finds himself living alone not through choice — as Thoreau did — but by circumstance.

I have a great deal of company in my house; especially in the morning, when nobody calls. Let me suggest a few comparisons, that some one may convey an idea of my situation. I am no more lonely than the loon in the pond that laughs so loud, or than Walden Pond itself. What company has that lonely lake, I pray? And yet it has not the blue devils, but the blue angels in it, in the azure tint of its waters. The sun is alone, except in thick weather, when there sometimes appear to be two, but one is a mock sun. God is alone, — but the devil, he is far from being alone; he sees a great deal of company: he is legion. I am sure more lonely than a single mullein or dandelion in a pasture, or a bean leaf, or sorrel, or a horse-fly, or a bumble-bee. I am no more lonely than the Mill Brook, or a weathercock, or the north star, or the south wind, or an April shower, or a January thaw, or the first spider in a new house.

Henry David Thoreau (1817 - 1862)

I never found the companion that was so companionable as solitude. We are for the most part more lonely when we go abroad among men than when we stay in our chambers. A man thinking or working is always alone, let him be where he will.

Henry David Thoreau

About the middle of September, 1941, young John Magee wrote a poem on the back of a letter that he mailed home to his parents in Washington, D.C. John was a pilot in the Royal Canadian Air Force.

John's father, the Reverend John G. Magee, was a Protestant Episcopal missionary. John had been born in China and spent most of his school days in England. He had earned the poetry prize at Rugby when he was sixteen. By the time he had completed his high school education at Avon, near Hartford, Connecticut, England was at war.

John had sworn never to fight or kill, but he had a deep love for England. He wanted to help. At the age of eighteen, he joined the Royal Canadian Air Force and returned to England as an officer with the 412th Squadron. In flight he found a joy he had never experienced anywhere else.

John saw his first enemy action in 1941. A month later, his plane collided with another Spitfire and both pilots were killed.

John Magee's poem "High Flight" is an eloquent expression of one man's conviction that we are never alone.

High Flight

Oh! I have slipped the surly bonds of Earth
And danced the skies on laughter-silvered wings;
Sunward I've climbed, and joined the tumbling mirth
Of sun-split clouds, and done a hundred things
You have not dreamed of: wheeled and soared and swung
High in the sunlit silence. Hov'ring there,
I've chased the shouting wind along, and flung
My eager craft through footless halls of air . . .
Up, up the long, delirious, burning blue
I've topped the wind-swept heights with easy grace,
Where never lark, or even eagle flew —
And, while with silent, lifting mind I've trod
The high untrespassed sanctity of space,
Put out my hand and touched the face of God.

John Magee (1922 - 1941)

Loss of sight came early in life to George Matheson of Glasgow, Scotland. By the time he was eighteen, he was almost totally blind. Nevertheless, he went on with his education and became an outstanding preacher and theologian of the Presbyterian church in Scotland. If Matheson's handicap discouraged him, it was not apparent to others, nor is it evident in the words to his hymn of faith, "O Love That Wilt Not Let Me Go."

O Love That Wilt Not Let Me Go

O Love that wilt not let me go,
I rest my weary soul in thee;
I give thee back the life I owe,
That in thine ocean depths its flow
May richer, fuller be.

O Light that followest all my way,
I yield my flickering torch to thee;
My heart restores its borrowed ray,
That in thy sunshine's blaze its day
May brighter, fairer be.

O Joy that seekest me through pain,
I cannot close my heart to thee;
I trace the rainbow through the rain,
And feel the promise is not vain
That morn shall tearless be.

O Cross that liftest up my head,
I dare not ask to fly from thee;
I lay in dust life's glory dead,
And from the ground there blossom's red
Life that shall endless be.

George Matheson (1842 - 1906)

PSALM 91

He that dwelleth in the secret place of the Most High shall abide under the shadow of the Almighty.

I will say of the Lord, He is my refuge and my fortress: my God: in him will I trust.

Surely he shall deliver thee from the snare of the fowler, and from the noisome pestilence.

He shall cover thee with his feathers, and under his wings shalt thou trust: his truth shall be thy shield and buckler.

Thou shalt not be afraid for the terror by night: nor for the arrow that flieth by day;

Nor for the pestilence that walketh in darkness; nor for the destruction that wasteth at noonday.

A thousand shall fall at thy side, and ten thousand at thy right hand: but it shall not come nigh thee.

Only with thine eyes shalt thou behold and see the reward of the wicked.

Because thou has made the Lord, which is my refuge, even the Most High, thy habitation:

There shall no evil befall thee, neither shall any plague come nigh thy dwelling.

For he shall give his angels charge over thee, to keep thee in all thy ways.

They shall bear thee up in their hands, lest thou dash thy foot against a stone.

Thou shalt tread upon the lion and adder: the young lion and the dragon shalt thou trample underfeet.

Because he hath set his love upon me, therefore will I deliver him: I will set him on high, because he hath known my name.

He shall call upon me, and I will answer him: I will be with him in trouble; I will deliver him, and honour him.

With long life will I satisfy him, and show him my salvation.

Come unto me, all ye that labour and are heavy laden, and I will give you rest.

Take my yoke upon you, and learn of me; for I am meek and lowly in heart: and ye shall find rest unto your souls.

For my yoke is easy, and my burden is light.

Matthew 11:28-30

A card on the dressing table of Gertrude Lawrence, the noted English actress, read:

"Anyone can carry his burden, however heavy, till nightfall. Anyone can do his work, however hard, for one day. Short horizons make life easier and give us one of the blessed secrets of grave, true, holy living."

. . . from PSALM 55

As for me, I will call upon God; and the Lord shall save me.

Evening, and morning, and at noon, will I pray, and cry aloud: and he shall hear my voice.

He hath delivered my soul in peace . . .

Cast thy burden upon the Lord, and he shall sustain thee: he shall never suffer the righteous to be moved . . .

A Psalm of David

. . . from PSALM 116

I love the Lord, because he hath heard my voice and my supplications.

Because he hath inclined his ear unto me, therefore will I call upon him as long as I live . . .

Return unto thy rest, O my soul: for the Lord hath dealt bountifully with thee.

For thou has delivered my soul from death, mine eyes from tears, and my feet from falling.

I will walk before the Lord in the land of the living.

I believed, therefore have I spoken: I was greatly afflicted: . . .

O Lord, truly I am thy servant: I am thy servant, and the son of thine handmaid: thou hast loosed my bonds.

I will offer to thee the sacrifice of thanksgiving, and will call upon the name of the Lord . . .

. . . Praise ye the Lord.

ALONE NO MORE

In 1865, Joseph Henry Gilmore was invited to preach at the Second Baptist Church in Rochester, New York. He opened the hymnal "to see what they were singing these days," and was astonished to find a hymn he himself had written and forgotten about: "He Leadeth Me: O Blessed Thought!"

The mystery was soon tracked down. In March, 1862, Gilmore had preached on the Twenty-Third Psalm at a prayer service in the First Baptist Church in Philadelphia. Following the service, he continued to meditate on the meaning of the psalm and composed the hymn on the back of the notes he had used for the evening. Then he gave it to his wife. She, in turn, submitted the verses to *Watchman and Reflector*, where it was published. Composer William B. Bradbury saw the poem and set it to music, after which it was soon published as a hymn.

He Leadeth Me: O Blessed Thought

He leadeth me: O blessed thought!
O words with heavenly comfort fraught!
Whate'er I do, where'er I be,
Still 'tis God's hand that leadeth me.

Sometimes mid scenes of deepest gloom,
Sometimes where Eden's bowers bloom,
By waters still, o'er troubled sea,
Still 'tis his hand that leadeth me.

Lord, I would place my hand in thine,
Nor ever murmur nor repine;
Content, whatever lot I see,
Since 'tis my God that leadeth me.

Refrain:
He leadeth me, he leadeth me,
By his own hand he leadeth me;
His faithful follower I would be,
For by his hand he leadeth me.

Joseph H. Gilmore (1834 - 1918)

Marjorie Hillis's *Live Alone and Like It* was a best seller in the 1930's. Following its publication, the author married but was soon widowed. As Marjorie Hillis Roulston, she wrote *You Can Start All Over*. In 1967, she added another book to her list. *Keep Going and Like It* is a small book of advice for lonely women in their sixties and following are some excerpts from it:

Fun should certainly take up some of one's time, but perhaps we'd better discuss Good Works first. (They can be fun too.) If you think this is stuffy, you might consider some women who have found it quite the opposite. One is the late Helen Menken, whose parents were deaf and who, as a result, had difficulty in learning to speak well as a small child. After her marriage, she gave regular time enthusiastically to helping foreigners or children with speech problems. One of New York's leading fashion designers gives some of her time to designing clothes for the handicapped at Dr. Howard Rusk's Rehabilitation Center. They're smart clothes too, though they may be reinforced under the arms where crutches would rub or have ingenious ways for the partially paralyzed to get in and out of them.

Another example is the editor of one of our well-known fashion magazines who gives her Sunday mornings to teaching horticulture in a mental institution. Still another woman who had a successful career in the fashion world before her marriage now spends one day a week making records of textbooks for the blind . . .

If you can't do any of these things, you can certainly do something, unless you're a poor helpless thing, in which case nobody will miss you. Fortunately, not many normally bright women are that today.

No matter where you are, there is certain to be some form of church work waiting to be done, and some charitable enterprise in need of help. Or if there isn't (which seems unlikely in even the most remote place) it's high time someone organized some, and why not you? This may take more doing than similar work in a larger place, but it will also be more rewarding. There's no place in the country where finding interests is impossible. If you live on the top of a mountain you might still find it fascinating to become an expert on trees or birds or wild life, or to revive the art of letter writing.

Marjorie Hillis Roulston

Deaf and blind from infancy, Helen Keller was a prisoner of her own handicaps until, at the age of seven, she began to learn to communicate with others. Once she was able to converse by sign language and read Braille, she could escape from her dark, silent prison.

Helen Keller regarded as a miracle her transition from an "unconscious clod of earth" to a soul who could receive knowledge. In a comparable way, she pointed out, people who have learned about God and follow Him are able to escape their own dull limitations and enter into another realm.

I had been sitting quietly in the library for half an hour. I turned to my teacher and said, 'Such a strange thing has happened! I have been far away all this time, and I haven't left the room.' What do you mean, Helen?' she asked, surprised. 'Why,' I cried, 'I have been in Athens.' Scarcely were the words out of my mouth when a bright, amazing realization seemed to catch my mind and set it ablaze. I perceived the realness of my soul and its sheer independence of all conditions of place and body. It was clear to me that it was because I was a spirit that I had so vividly 'seen' and felt a place thousands of miles away. Space was nothing to spirit!

In that new consciousness shone the Presence of God, Himself a Spirit everywhere at once, the Creator dwelling in all the universe simultaneously. The fact that my little soul could reach out over continents and seas to Greece, despite a blind, deaf, and stumbling body, sent another exulting emotion rushing over me. I had broken through my limitations and found in touch an eye. I could read the thoughts of wise men — thoughts which had for ages survived their mortal life, and could possess them as part of myself.

If this were true, how much more could God, the uncircumscribed Spirit, cancel the harms of nature — accident, pain, destruction — and reach out to his children. Deafness and blindness, then, were of no real account. They were relegated to the outer circle of my life.

Helen Keller (1880 - 1968)

Sadness, loneliness, melancholy — call it what you will — the feeling is not peculiar to any day or age. Charles Boswell, the 18th Century biographer, had a knack for stimulating that famous man of letters, Dr. Samuel Johnson, to talk. In his *The Life of Samuel Johnson*, Boswell recalls a conversation dealing with melancholy:

Upon our arrival at Oxford, Dr. Johnson and I . . . were disappointed on finding that one of the fellows, his friend Mr. Scott . . . was gone to the country. We put up at the Angel Inn, and passed the evening by ourselves in easy and familiar conversation. Talking of melancholy, he (Johnson) observed, "A man so afflicted, Sir, must divert distressing thoughts, and not combat with them." *Boswell:* "May he not think them down, Sir?" *Johnson:* "No, Sir. To attempt to *think them down* is madness. He should have a lamp constantly burning in his bed-chamber during the night, and if wakefully disturbed, take a book, and read, and compose himself to rest. To have the management of the mind is a great art, and it may be attained in a considerable degree by experience and habitual exercise." *Boswell:* "Should not he provide amusements for himself? Would it not, for instance, be right for him to take a course of chymistry?" *Johnson:* "Let him take a course of chymistry, or a course of rope-dancing or a course of anything to which he is inclined at the time. Let him contrive to have as many retreats for his mind as he can, as many things to which it can fly from itself . . ."

In the year 1833, the *Cone Ruggiero*, a small sailing ship engaged in carrying oranges from Palermo, Italy to Marseilles, France, was becalmed in the Straits of Bonifacio. A young English clergyman, John Henry Newman, was aboard the ship as a passenger. He was returning from a trip to Sicily where he had been seriously ill. Others had despaired of his recovery, but Newman had never doubted for a moment that he would survive. He was convinced that God had work for him to do.

For a week, the sails of the small vessel hung slack. Newman, although still weak from his illness, spent his time writing poetry. One of the poems was "Lead, Kindly Light," and the words became the hymn that is famous throughout the Christian world. It was Newman's statement of his faith that God would direct his life.

Newman converted to Roman Catholicism in 1845, became a priest, and in 1879 was elected Cardinal.

Lead, Kindly Light

Lead, kindly Light, amid the encircling gloom,
    Lead thou me on;
The night is dark, and I am far from home;
    Lead thou me on:
Keep thou my feet; I do not ask to see
The distant scene; one step enough for me.

I was not ever thus, nor prayed that thou
    Shouldst lead me on:
I loved to choose and see my path: but now
    Lead thou me on.
I loved the garish day, and spite of fears,
Pride ruled my will; remember not past years.

So long thy power hath blest me, sure it still
    Will lead me on
O'er moor and fen, o'er crag and torrent, till
    The night is gone.
And with the morn those angel faces smile
Which I have loved long since, and lost awhile.

John Henry Newman (1801 - 1890)

Richard E. Byrd's decision to remain alone at the Advance Weather Base throughout the antarctic winter of 1934 would have been perilous under the best of circumstances. But conditions were far from the best. For one thing, he was a prisoner of the ice with only a hand-cranked radio for communication. For another, the stove, necessary to keep Byrd from freezing to death in a temperature continually below zero, proved to be his chief enemy. It gave off noxious fumes.

Carbon monoxide is a silent killer — a gas with no tell-tale odor. Byrd was already ill before he realized the cause of his discomfort. In the paragraphs that follow, Byrd relates how he managed to discipline his mind so that he could survive the crisis. Byrd's isolation was real, but those who have found themselves set apart from society in other ways may find a parallel in their own lives.

To begin with, there were two certainties. One was that no help was to be had from the outside — the Barrier was a wall between. The other was that little could be done about improving ventilation in the shack. Even if materials had been available to make a drastic change, I was palpably too weak to undertake anything of that order. Here the warmish weather (the temperature had risen to $-22°$ F.) had been an unexpected ally. I had been able to do without the stove for long intervals during the day; and the relief from the fumes had given my body respite. This was sheer luck, however. The greatest cold was yet to come, and might come any day.

These were facts. To the degree that a man is superior to his destiny, I should be able to rise above them. Few men during their lifetime come anywhere near exhausting the resources dwelling within them. There are deep wells of strength that are never used. Could I find a way to tap those physical potentialities locked up within myself? Well, suppose I were able to. It still wouldn't mean a great deal. Clearly, my remaining material resources couldn't be very much. Therefore I must find other sources of replenishment. In such times, when the tricks and expediencies of cornered men fall to pieces in their hands, they turn to God — as I did, after my fashion.

. . . being a practical man, I recognized a big difference between the mere affirmation of faith and its effective implementation. To desire harmony, or peace, or whatever word you care to give to the sense of identification with the orderly processes of life, would be a step in the right direction: but this by itself was not enough. *I had to work for it.* Above everything else, what I sought must be logical: it must be brought about by following the laws of nature. It didn't occur to me to formulate a prayer. I would express whatever urge to pray I had in action — besides, the sheer hunger to live was prayer enough . . .

. . . To survive, I must continue to husband my strength, doing whatever had to be done in the simplest manner possible and without strain. I must sleep and eat and build up strength. To

avoid further poisoning from the fumes, I must use the stove sparingly and the gasoline pressure lantern not at all.

So much for the practical procedure . . . Something more — the will and desire to endure these hardships — was necessary. They must come from deep inside me. But how? By taking control of my thought. By extirpating all lugubrious ideas the instant they appeared and dwelling only on those conceptions which would make for peace. A discordant mind, black with confusion and despair, would finish me off as thoroughly as the cold. Discipline of this sort is not easy.

. . . The dark side of a man's mind seems to be a sort of antenna tuned to catch gloomy thoughts from all directions. I found it so with mine. That was an evil night. It was as if all the world's vindictiveness were concentrated upon me as upon a personal enemy. I sank to depths of disillusionment which I had not believed possible. It would be tedious to discuss them. Misery, after all, is the tritest of emotions. All that need be said is that eventually my faith began to make itself felt; and by concentrating on it and reaffirming the truth about the universe as I saw it, I was able again to fill my mind with the fine and comforting things of the world that had seemed irretrievably lost.

Richard E. Byrd

. . . I am deeply touched by individuals who may have some physical handicap or condition of suffering that makes them feel alienated. The little boy with thick glasses who wistfully stands by as classmates tussle over a football; the young mother struck with an invaliding disease, who from a wheelchair must watch her children grow up; the face of the older man, just retired by his company, sitting on a bench where he cannot be seen, but where he can see his friends dash to make the 8:04 train into town. These and so many others, who seem to be in a special area of loneliness, prompt my tender and questioning concern.

I cannot pretend to have answers for all these people. Theirs may be a loneliness that my most sympathetic imagination cannot touch. But this I do know: that never, never, never are all the doors shut. The most important door of all, that one within your own aloneness, can be closed only by you. If some physical limitation cuts you off from most of life, there may be presented an opportunity to open those precious doors more widely than ever before. Many people have walked through those broader arches and enriched the ages with scientific discoveries, poetry, songs, and wisdom. It can be so with you.

Lowell Russell Ditzen

For the thinking, alert person, there is always a substitute for the dearest treasure lost. I know women who, to fill their minds with creative thoughts, have taken courses in languages, studied stenography, flower-arranging, started small businesses in their homes. I know others who, in a sort of helpless despair, have sunk deeper and deeper into the mire of their own negative thinking. The latter are the ones who keep the doctors' waiting rooms full.

Mary Margaret McBride

Solitude is fine but you need someone to tell you that solitude is fine.

Honore de Balzac (1799 - 1850)

Solitude makes us tougher toward ouselves and tenderer toward others: in both ways, it improves our character.

Friedrich Nietzsche (1844 - 1900)

PSALM 46

God is our refuge and strength, a very present help in trouble.

Therefore will not we fear, though the earth be removed, and though the mountains be carried into the midst of the sea;

Though the waters thereof roar and be troubled, though the mountains shake with the swelling thereof. Selah.

There is a river, the streams whereof shall make glad the city of God, the holy place of the tabernacles of the Most High.

God is in the midst of her; she shall not be moved: God shall help her, and that right early.

The heathen raged, the kingdoms were moved: he uttered his voice, the earth melted.

The Lord of hosts is with us; the God of Jacob is our refuge. Selah.

Come, behold the works of the Lord, what desolations he hath made in the earth.

He maketh wars to cease unto the end of the earth: he breaketh the bow, and cutteth the spear in sunder: he burneth the chariot in the fire.

Be still, and know that I am God: I will be exalted among the heathen, I will be exalted in the earth.

The Lord of hosts is with us: the God of Jacob is our refuge. Selah

When you close your doors, and
make darkness within, remember
never to say that you are alone,
for you are not alone; nay, God is
within, and your genius is within.
And what need have they of light
to see what you are doing?

Epictetus (60? - 120? AD)

And who was Epictetus? What did he know about loneliness and imprisonment? He was the son of a Roman slave and therefore, according to Roman law, destined himself to be a slave also.

Epictetus was passed from one owner to another until he finally reached Epaphroditus, in the Emperor Nero's court. Epaphroditus had once been a slave himself and he compassionately allowed Epitetus to attend lectures and to educate himself, and then freed him.

Epictetus had apparently been mistreated in his youth for he was frail and lame, yet he was still able to face the world with remarkable cheerfulness. Of imprisonment he said, "It is only my body that you imprison." He believed that even slaves or prisoners could be spirtually free.

"Seek not that everything should happen as you wish," Epictetus also said, "but wish for everything to happen as it actually does happen, and you will be serene."

Be Still, My Soul

Be still, my soul: the Lord is on thy side:
Bear patiently the cross of grief or pain:
Leave to thy God to order and provide:
In every change he faithful will remain.
Be still, my soul: thy best, thy heavenly friend
Through thorny ways leads to a joyful end.

Be still, my soul: thy God doth undertake
To guide the future as he has the past.
Thy hope, thy confidence let nothing shake;
All now mysterious shall be bright at last.
Be still, my soul: the waves and winds still know
His voice who ruled them while he dwelt below.

Be still, my soul: the hour is hastening on
When we shall be forever with the Lord,
When disappointment, grief, and fear are gone,
Sorrow forgot, love's purest joys restored.
Be still, my soul: when change and tears are past,
All safe and blessed we shall meet at last.

Katherina von Schlegel (b. 1697)
Translated by Jane Borthwick

Expecting to go through life with
no loneliness whatever is like
expecting to escape all illness and
disappointments. A little
loneliness doesn't hurt anyone
and sometimes it is definitely
helpful in the end.

Marjorie Hillis

God of the Ages, by Whose Hand

God of the ages, by whose hand
Through years long past our lives were led,
Give us new courage now to stand,
New faith to find the paths ahead.

Thou art the thought beyond all thought,
The gift beyond our utmost prayer;
No farthest reach where thou are not,
No height but we may find thee there.

Forgive our wavering trust in thee,
Our wild alarms, our trembling fears;
In thy strong hand eternally
Rests the unfolding of the years.

Though there be dark, uncharted space.
With worlds on worlds beyond our sight,
Still may we trust thy love and grace,
And wait thy word, Let there be light.

Elisabeth Burrowes (1885 -   )

Not in the achievement, but in
the endurance of the human soul,
does it show its divine grandeur,
and its alliance with the infinite
God.

Edwin Hubbel Chapin

Speak to Him thou for He hears, and spirit with
   spirit can meet —
Closer is He than breathing, and nearer than
   hands and feet.

Alfred, Lord Tennyson

I take Thy hand, and fears grow still;
   Behold Thy face, and doubts remove;
Who would not yield his wavering will
   To perfect Truth and boundless Love?

Samuel Johnson

You may be whatever you resolve to be. Determine to be something in the world, and you will be something. "I cannot," never accomplished anything; "I will try," has wrought wonders.

Joel Hawes

Either I will find a way, or I will make one.

Sir Philip Sidney

Strength does not come from physical capacity. It comes from an indomitable will.

Mahatma Gandhi

"The Everlasting Arms." I think of that whenever rest is sweet. How the whole earth and the strength of it, that is almightiness, is beneath every tired creature to give it rest; *holding* us, always! No thought of God is closer than that. No human tenderness of patience is greater than that which gathers in its arms a little child, and holds it, heedless of weariness. And He fills the great earth, and all upon it, with this unseen force of His love, that never forgets or exhausts itself, so that everywhere we may lie down in His bosom, and be comforted.

Adeline D. T. Whitney

Strength is born in the deep silence of long-suffering hearts; not amidst joy.

Felicia Dorothea Browne Hemans

When every hope is gone, "when helpers fail and comforts flee," I find that help arrives somehow, from I know not where. Supplication, worship, prayer are no superstitions; they are acts more real than the acts of eating, drinking, sitting or walking. It is no exaggeration to say that they alone are real, all else is unreal.

Mahatma Gandhi

In all things it is better to hope than to despair.

Johann Wolfgang von Goethe

God Will Take Care of You

Be not dismayed whate'er betide,
God will take care of you;
Beneath his wings of love abide,
God will take care of you.

Through days of toil when heart doth fail,
God will take care of you;
When dangers fierce your path assail,
God will take care of you.

All you may need he will provide,
God will take care of you;
Nothing you ask will be denied,
God will take care of you.

No matter what may be the test,
God will take care of you;
Lean, weary one, upon his breast,
God will take care of you.

Refrain:
God will take care of you
Through every day; o'er all the way;
He will take care of you,
God will take care of you.

Civilla D. Martin (1869 - 1948)

Loneliness . . . is and always has
been the central and inevitable
experience of every man.

Thomas Wolfe (1900 - 1938)

Acknowledgments

The editor and the publisher have made every effort to trace the ownership of all copyrighted material and to secure permission from copyright holders of such material. In the event of any question arising as to the use of any material the publisher and editor, while expressing regret for inadvertent error, will be pleased to make the necessary corrections in future printings. Thanks are due to the following authors, publishers, publications and agents for permission to use the material indicated.

DOUBLEDAY & COMPANY, INC., for excerpt from *Keep Going and Like It* by Marjorie Hillis Roulston, copyright © 1967 by Marjorie Hillis Roulston.

FARRAR, STRAUS & GIROUX, INC., for excerpt from *Carrying the Fire* by Michael Collies, copyright © 1974 by Michael Collins.

HARCOURT BRACE JOVANOVICH, INC., for "Courage" from *Last Flight* by Amelia Earhart, copyright 1937 by George Palmer Putnam; renewed 1965 by Mrs. George Palmer Putnam; for excerpt from *Hour of Gold, Hour of Lead* by Anne Morrow Lindbergh, copyright © 1973 by Anne Morrow Lindbergh.

HAWTHORN BOOKS, INC., for excerpt from *And Now To Live Again* by Betsey Barton.

HOLT, RINEHART AND WINSTON, for excerpt from *You Are Never Alone* by Lowell Russell Ditzen, copyright © 1956 by Holt, Rinehart and Winston, Publishers.

ALFRED A. KNOPF, INC., for excerpts from *Markings* by Dag Hammarskjold translated by Leif Sjoberg and W. H. Auden, copyright © 1964 by Alfred A. Knopf, Inc. and Faber and Faber Ltd.

G. P. PUTNAM'S SONS, for excerpt from *Alone* by Richard E. Byrd, copyright 1938 by Richard E. Byrd, renewed © 1966 by Marie A. Byrd.

THE RODEHEAVER CO., for "In the Garden" by C. Austin Miles, copyright 1912 by Hall-Mack Co., renewed 1940 (extended) by The Rodeheaver Co., Owner.

SWEDENBORG FOUNDATION, INC., for excerpt from *My Religion* by Helen Keller, copyright 1974 by Swedenborg Foundation, Inc.